THE B SEA CAPTAIN

**PYRFORD PRIMARY SCHOOL
COLDHARBOUR ROAD
PYRFORD, WOKING
SURREY GU22 8SP**

*Written by Denis Bond
Illustrated by Martin Remphry*

Collins Educational
An Imprint of HarperCollins*Publishers*

The sea captain was well-known in the town where he lived. He was always telling fantastic stories to his friends and neighbours.

Most people were fed up with the stories as they'd heard them so many times before. And they were sure that the stories weren't true. They were sure that the sea captain was telling great big fibs.

One morning, the sea captain went to the fish shop.
"I'll have that large kipper for my lunch," he said.
The fishmonger smiled.
"Why don't you catch your own fish when you're out at sea?" he asked.

"Because it's very dangerous catching fish," replied the sea captain. "I once caught a huge shark on the end of my fishing line. It was a very angry-looking shark, with long, sharp teeth and enormous jaws. It was very, very strong. Almost as strong as me!"

"You've told me this story a dozen times before," sighed the fishmonger.

But the sea captain took no notice of him and carried on: "The shark pulled me overboard and I had to wrestle with it under the water," he said. "Over and over we rolled. I wasn't scared at all. I grabbed the shark by its pointed nose and dragged it through the waves. It was *terrified*! I won the fight, of course, because I'm *so* brave."

Next, the brave sea captain went to the greengrocer's.
"I'll have half of that large cabbage to eat with my kipper," he said.
The greengrocer reached for her long knife to cut the cabbage in two.
"I once had a knife like that," said the sea captain. "Well... it was a *sword*, actually," he added. "It came in very handy when pirates decided to invade my ship."

"You've told me this story a hundred times already," tutted the greengrocer.
"There were *thousands* of them, and my crew ran away in fear," the sea captain went on. "But not me! I fought every one of those pirates single-handedly with my sword. They were *terrified*! I was *very* brave, I must admit."

Later, the brave sea captain went to the park to feed the ducks. The park keeper was feeding the ducks too. "Aren't they handsome creatures?" sighed the park keeper. "I really love my ducks."

"If you think ducks are handsome creatures," said the sea captain, "you ought to see *dolphins*. I once had *hundreds* of dolphins surrounding my ship. Now, they really are handsome creatures."
"You've told me this story a thousand times already," grumbled the park keeper.

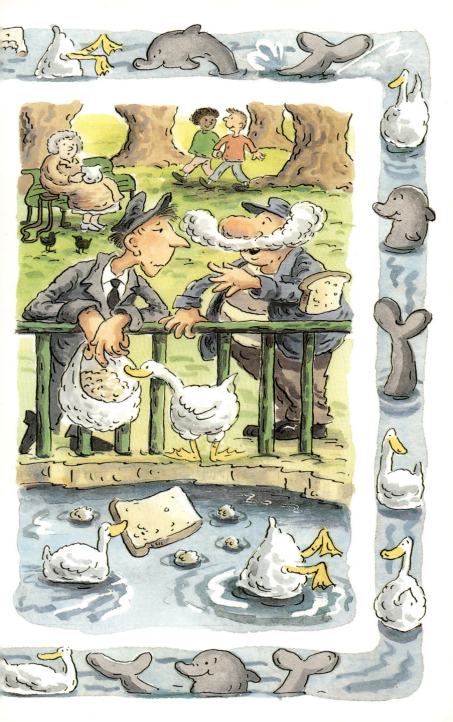

"I dived into the water and climbed onto a dolphin's back," the sea captain went on.
"He took me for a *wonderful* ride. All of the dolphins were leaping in and out of the waves. My dolphin leapt so high he nearly touched the sun. Most people would have been scared stiff. But not me! That's because I'm *very, very* brave."

As the brave sea captain left the park, he noticed a man working on his allotment. The man was digging potatoes. The sea captain peered at him through the railings.

"If you dig deep enough," called out the sea captain, "you might come across a casket of hidden treasure." "Not the casket of hidden treasure story again!" sighed the man. "You've told me that story a million times already!"

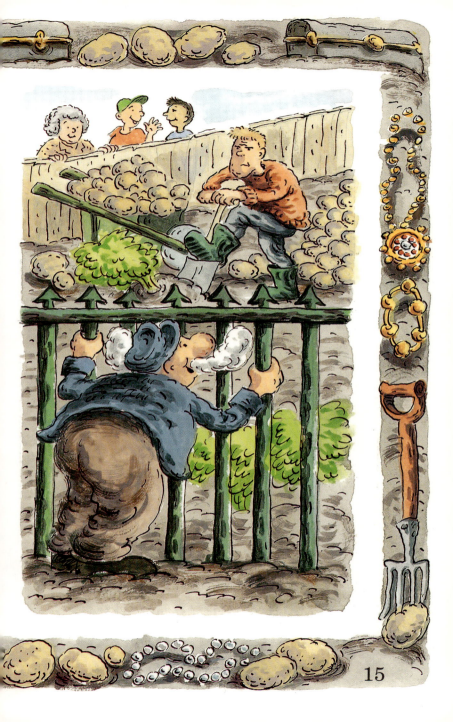

The sea captain ignored him: "I was in this dark cave on a desert island," he went on. "And I found this casket full of bracelets and necklaces and precious jewels. I didn't know that I was being watched by some terrifying sea monsters who lived in the dark cave!"

"Suddenly, they all charged at me, growling and gnashing their big, pointed teeth. One of them grabbed my shirt in its huge jaws and ripped it from my back. I had to leave all the treasure behind and run back to my ship."
"That wasn't very brave, was it?" said the man.
"Er... no," stammered the sea captain. He blushed. "But I *am* a very fast runner," he added.

Back at home, after a delicious lunch of kipper and cabbage, the sea captain was sitting by the fire, whistling an old sea ditty, when he heard a tap at the window. He looked up and saw the face of an old woman, grinning at him.

"I want to go to sea," she cried eagerly. "It sounds great fun. Can I go to sea with you?"

"Follow me," said the sea captain proudly, and he led the old woman down towards the harbour, where there were lots of boats. "This is mine," said the captain, rather sheepishly. "But this is just a little ferry boat!" exclaimed the old woman. "Surely you can't sail to sea in *this*!"

The sea captain was just about to confess that he'd been telling huge fibs; that he wasn't *really* a sea captain... that he was just a ferry boat captain, when a sudden gust of wind blew them off their feet and onto the deck.

A great crack of lightning split the sky and rain began to pour down.
"Shiver me timbers!" shrieked the ferry boat captain. "Hold on tight, my dear. We're about to face a terrific storm!"

The ferry boat was lifted high on the waves as the storm lashed across its bow. Up and down it went. Up and down. Up and down.

"I feel sick," groaned the old woman.
"You'll be all right in a minute," the captain assured her.

Soon, the wind and the waves had carried the ferry boat far out to sea.
"I'm frightened!" cried the old woman.
"Don't worry," said the captain. "I'll look after you. I'm not frightened. I'm *very, very* brave."

Finally the storm died down. The sun came out and the sea was as calm as the duck-pond in the park.

The old woman leaned over the boat's rail.

"Look!" she cried, excitedly. "Fish! Can we catch one, do you think?"

The captain quickly hurled himself across the deck and dragged the old woman away from the rail.

"Come away!" he yelled. "You might fall overboard. And the sharks might eat you!"

The boat sailed on and on until, through his telescope, the ferry boat captain spied dry land.
"Land ahoy!" he shouted.
"Is it a desert island?" asked the old woman, excitedly. "A desert island with caves and monsters and caskets of hidden treasure?"
"Not quite," laughed the captain.

They left the boat and scrambled up the beach, startling all the sunbathers in their deck chairs, until they reached the promenade.
"The seaside! I love the seaside," laughed the old woman.
"I haven't been to the seaside for years!"
"Me neither," smiled the captain.

The windows of the souvenir shop were full of wonderful presents. There were earrings and bracelets and necklaces full of sparkling chips of coloured glass.

"I'd like to buy something special," said the old woman. She took her purse out of her handbag and paid for a beautiful, sparkling necklace. It was very cheap, but it looked *very* expensive.
"I like that," grinned the ferry boat captain, as they crossed the road and headed back towards the beach. "It looks very pretty on you."

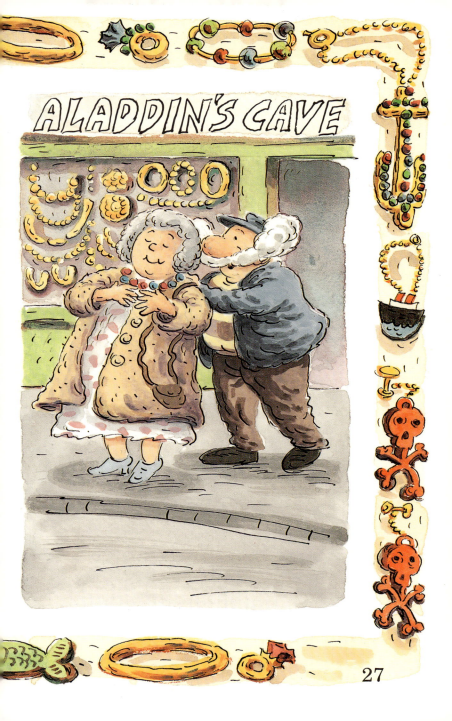

Suddenly, they saw two men wearing large, golden earrings, speeding towards them on a motorbike. As the bike zoomed past, one of the men lunged forwards and tried to snatch the necklace from around the old woman's neck. But the captain was too quick for them.

He bravely whisked the old woman to one side, and sent one of the rascals reeling with a punch.

"We were nearly robbed!" gasped the old woman, as the bike sped off into the distance.

Later, as the ferry boat sailed home, the captain looked very worried. He was sure the old woman would tell *everyone* in the town that the sea captain wasn't a sea captain at all! He was just the captain of a very small ferry boat.

But...

"The captain saved me from fish that might have eaten me," said the old woman.

"Mmm... sharks," they all said, knowingly.

"And he saved me from robbers with large, golden earrings."

"Mmm... pirates!" they all mumbled.

"It was such fun being with the sea captain," said the old woman. "I hope you all realise how brave he is."

"Oh, we do!" everyone agreed.
"He's *very, very* brave."

"Tell us that story about the huge shark on your fishing line," said the fishmonger.
"And the one about the pirates," added the greengrocer.

The sea captain winked at the old woman... and he began, once again, to tell his stories.